The Easy Way to Write Short Stories That Sell

Rob Parnell

Я&R

The Easy Way to Write Short Stories That Sell

First published by R&R Books Film Music

An Я&R Production

PO Box 485
Morphett Vale SA 5162
info@rnrbooksfilmmusic.com.au

ISBN: 1499373236
ISBN: 978-1499373233

DEDICATION

To Robyn. Thank you for everything:

for believing, for being gorgeous, for lovin' me...

CONTENTS

FOREWORD

Hi, my name is Rob Parnell.

First off, this book is designed to ensure that you start writing short stories that will soon be published. It is also meant as an introduction to the writer's life. If you need motivation, inspiration or for some reason you are blocked, you've come to the right place.

Now, let me tell you a little about myself, so you can get some perspective on what to expect from this book on the easy way to write short stories that sell.

I've been a professional writer for more than a decade. I've sold around two-hundred-and-forty-thousand e-books and courses, been on various bestseller charts, best website lists, and generally done pretty well. I also surprised the heck out of myself (and my wife) by becoming wealthy in the process.

I don't say any of this to brag, only to emphasize the fact I've done all this without having a publishing deal, a literary agent or any other kind of third-party backing.

Fact is, I was dead broke in 1998, when I had a proper job, back in what I now refer to as the *Dark Days*. But I managed to turn all that around when I decided to become a professional writer. Now, I'm just one of a new breed who make a comfortable living as an independent author, something that could not have happened, I'm pretty sure, had it not been for the Internet.

Writers are in a unique position these days. We can control our destinies in a way that was impossible just twenty, perhaps even ten, years ago. No longer do we have to rely on the whims of faceless corporations to create a paid writing career for ourselves. We don't have to wait around for publishers and agents to respond to our submissions, usually in the negative. And we don't have to spend long periods - years sometimes - awaiting release and distribution by traditional publishers and hanging on like grim death for royalties that may or may not provide enough for us to live on.

Nowadays we can do it all ourselves. Not only that, we can publish our work quickly, see more or less instant results, and get earnings within weeks instead of years, and all this without having to split our royalties with anyone who might stand between our fans and our work.

But as *Spider Man's* dad said, *With great power comes great responsibility!*

It might be easier to publish our own work than ever before, but we still have an important duty to make sure our work is highly polished - and to do that ourselves, rather than rely on others to do it for us.

For the last twelve plus years I've run a website called the *Easy Way to Write:* www.easywaytowrite.com. (Go there online for free writing lessons.)

Upwards of a million subscribers have passed through my website, and perhaps a thousand times that as visitors. This is all the more remarkable because you've probably never heard of me!

As a shy, retiring sort of bloke, like most writers, I've shunned the limelight and just got on with doing what I do best: writing.

Since 2002, when I first began my online presence, it's been my calling and privilege to help and inspire writers of all levels to constantly improve their writing style and technique.

But just improving as a writer is not always enough. Right?

We need money to live on - to give us the freedom to write. If we write and no cash comes in, then we're not going to last very long, no matter how passionate we are about our craft. If we don't achieve solid monetary success as a writer, we'll end up working nine-to-five, again, just to pay the rent or the mortgage and all those pesky bills.

Most wannabe authors harbor the dream that one day they might make a living as a writer. So, in order to do my bit to help in the realization of that dream, I've made it my mission to help writers earn money.

And I like to think, through my books and courses, that I help writers become more *commercially* successful. Much of my teaching is slanted towards the production of salable writing as opposed to simply creating better writing for its own sake.

Yes. I want my writing students to reap the rewards of independent authorship and make a good living from being a fiction writer. Because, rather than just focus on improving a writer's self-image, or appeal to his or her desire to practice the perfecting of the craft, I prefer to zone in on helping writers create commercial fiction (short stories and novels) that can openly compete in the marketplace.

Because when writers make money from their writing, they are *validated*.

They have positive proof they're not wasting their time.

The motivation to write and complete works can sometimes be hard to come by. Many would-be writers suffer blocks brought about by self-doubt and other, often illusory, handicaps. I try very hard, in my writing courses and books, to provide motivation and techniques that induce 'self-support' because I think this is half the battle we writers have to overcome when faced with long periods alone in front of a computer screen: just getting on with it. Doing it. And completing the projects we start.

However, it's clear that getting paid to write is going to be a much more powerful motivator in the long term!

And that's what I want for you, my friend.

I want you to read this book, absorb its teachings and get yourself out there - and start selling your short stories. For money.

Over the last decade, I have produced twenty-eight writing courses and self-help manuals. I've written almost one-thousand online articles and blogs. Along the way, I've penned numerous short stories, many of which have been published in magazines and anthologies, all over the world.

This book is designed to help you get your own short stories published.

You see, for around twenty years I wrote short stories with very little success. Then, when I discovered the techniques I'm about to teach you in this book, I began to get almost *every* story I wrote published. Not because I was famous or particularly brilliant at writing - but because I finally understood what was required of me by short story publishers.

It's All About Mindset

I consider myself a writer, as you may have guessed. I also consider myself a *professional* writer. Even though, a few years back, anyone who essentially self-published their own books was not usually afforded this title - or indeed taken seriously by other professional writers.

Until now.

The publishing landscape is changing. And this change has in no small way been caused and precipitated by online writers. By people like you and me - writers who have grown tired of waiting for validation and endorsement by monolithic corporations whose only interest is in their revenue stream.

It was touch and go for us for a while.

Back in the last millennium, I submitted countless short stories and a couple of novels to publishers far and wide, in a bid for acceptance. (Funny how that word has a double meaning.) For the most part, the results were, predictably perhaps, depressing.

Serial rejection - and the attendant feelings of unworthiness - set in. And I, like thousands of other authors, grew older with a sometimes overwhelming feeling that I may never be good enough to sell my books and stories to the public.

For a long while, I struggled. Actually right up until around 2000, when I first took my potential career as a writer seriously enough to begin to do it properly.

A short diversion into history... maybe you can relate.

I wrote my first short story when I was five years old. It was about a young boy who planned a raid on a local sweet shop... nothing autobiographical of course! Just a youthful fantasy.

At primary school, when I was asked to record what we did during the holidays, I invariably wrote about things that never happened: describing how, for example, I was abducted by aliens or went on a trip down the Amazon to find lost treasure. My teachers soon realized that, if I wasn't delusional, I was probably going to end up a fiction writer...

I continued to write sometimes epic fictional creations throughout my school-life, usually stories that I didn't have time to finish but that extended to forty or fifty pages for a three-page assignment - much to the glee of my favorite English teachers who often embarrassed the hell out of me by reading my literary efforts to the class. This was something that was not always good for your health in an all boys school where writing prowess was considered a flaw that needed to be - sometimes literally - beaten out of you by your classmates!

During my teens I became convinced I should be an artist of some sort - dreaming of being rich and famous - despite the fact my mother thought this was a disastrous decision that should be discouraged at all costs.

After school, life got in the way, of course. I continued to write but without much success until, when working nine-to-five became completely unbearable, I decided to do something about my dream to become a professional writer.

In 2000 I began to write short stories with a committed view to getting them published. I joined a writers' group and duly produced a story a week to be read out in the group. We shared our successes and rejections. What I noticed fairly early on was that, if you write a story and then submit it to a magazine, you rarely got it accepted.

BUT, if you studied the magazine FIRST - and got to know exactly what the editor liked - and THEN wrote the story FOR the magazine, you invariably got the story published.

This is part of what you need to understand when you read this book.

Success at writing is not just about becoming a better writer - or of somehow being good enough to be published.

No, becoming a paid writer is about having the correct mindset.

It's about knowing what people need and expect from your writing. It's about using your skill to give people what they want. This is the real trick to writing anything that will sell. You have the target audience in your mind as you write. You need to care about your readers - and be perceptive of their needs. When you're a professional, you're not just writing for your amusement. You're writing to be *read*. This simple truth can be an epiphany for many writers. It was for me and I hope it will be for you.

When I finally realized that the writing was not about me, I became a professional. And I haven't looked back since.

To me, writing is not just a hobby or an idle past-time. It is a way of life, a way of seeing the world, constantly trying to understand it and reacting appropriately to it.

It's about helping others to see more clearly through our writing. It's about helping yourself to see more clearly - and relating that improved vision to others.

To me, becoming a better writer is about becoming a better person. It is about changing your life for the better, being independent in thought and action, taking responsibility for your life and creating a lifestyle that positively supports a successful writer's mission.

In the old days a writer was someone who was often poor, writing in a garret somewhere, struggling over words without money. Thankfully, all that has changed. You can now be a writer - and get paid, independent of arbitrary restrictions.

To me, the *Easy Way to Write* is not just a website, or a snappy name to help sell books, it is a philosophy, and a way of thinking - a success mindset. Much of my work focuses on how to get writers in the right headspace for creating great work quickly and easily - and becoming successful enough to enjoy the benefits and perks that go with the lifestyle a writer can attain easily with commitment and persistence.

And so, here's one book I know will help you in achieving your goals, personal and professional.

Writing short stories is probably the best way to hone your craft as a writer.

And with this book, I present what I believe is the easiest way to proceed on your journey to writing success.

Keep Writing!

Rob Parnell

INTRODUCTION

Welcome, fellow writer!

If you've ever submitted short stories for publication you may have gotten disillusioned very quickly. Even after lots of hard work, mental dexterity and painstaking editing, it's possible you've received many rejections and wondered whether it was all worth it.

Well, I'm here to tell you that it is, and, even if you've been serially rejected up to this point, you may not have realized just how close you were to an acceptance.

Because, yes, getting short stories published is about persistence but it's also imperative you get your submissions *exactly right* for your target markets.

This book will outline what the requirements are and describe precisely how to construct the kind of stories editors want to publish.

This book is not just about giving you the basics of good writing. No, I aim to give you much more specific advice, based on the experience of the many hundreds of published authors I have worked with over the years, as well as including my own knowledge of getting stories into print.

While there may never be a precise formula to getting published for everyone, there *is* a surefire way of being taken seriously, as an individual, by editors and publishers.

There is no mysterious Masonic club you must join, or any secret knowledge you need to acquire. Editors are in no way trying to make it impossible for you to compete. Nor do they behave in a way that is hard to understand.

Actually, editors are fairly predictable. They're basically looking for the same things - over and over - in a good short story when they first look at a manuscript submission.

* *Excellent presentation.*

* *An interesting mind at work*

* A thorough grasp of the rules of writing

They know, even from just a cursory glance, that when these three criteria are in evidence, a good short story is almost inevitable. Which story an editor picks from the hundreds to choose from is then down to the requirements of the particular publication and his/her personal preference.

It may surprise you to learn that, for an editor, finding the above three qualities is the easy part of the job. Many writers fail to present their stories well. It's estimated that around 97% of all short story submissions are badly formatted, contain basic spelling and grammar mistakes and show that the author has little understanding or respect for punctuation. Little wonder so many stories are rejected.

Editors generally weed out this 97% by reading the opening paragraph. If there are errors in evidence, the editor will simply dump the story in the bin - or in the return file. Life's too short to read badly presented work. An editor's experience tells him or her that, if there are errors early on, the story will unerringly not satisfy. There's no need to read the whole story to know that. If a writer can't get the first paragraph right, there's little hope for the rest of the story.

You simply cannot afford to ignore the rules of good grammar, punctuation and spelling when submitting manuscripts. You might think I'm stating the obvious but, after teaching writing professionally for over twelve years I am constantly amazed by most writers' cavalier attitude to this most fundamental of issues.

As a matter of course, make a commitment to continually familiarize yourself with what's considered good writing technique. Get hold of a copy of *The Elements of Style* by William Strunk, still the byword on acceptable English usage. Or, consider taking one of my courses on self-editing. Or, just take a look at a good dictionary. Most will have an introduction, many of which contain a short section on the rules of good writing.

That said, and I hope you fully appreciate the importance of presentation above all else, you may now proceed with this book. If you absorb my teaching, I guarantee your work will be in the top three-percent of viable manuscript submissions. Then, I'm sure you'll be seeing your stories in print in no time.

PART ONE:

MINDSET

Mental Preparation

Before you venture into writing proper, it's important to have the right mindset.

Often, writers are good starters but poor finishers. Too frequently, writers respond to an overwhelming compulsion to write without making appropriate plans to ensure a positive outcome. This is why writers get 'stuck' or 'blocked' and can't or don't know how to complete their stories.

Mental preparation is therefore vitally important.

Before you start your short story, you should spend time focusing on the belief that you really can finish it. This may require some degree of meditation and visualization. If that sounds too new-age for you, call it 'talking to yourself' if you prefer.

You need to convince your subconscious mind that you are a good writer, and that you are going to write and finish a great short story. Do this by making positive affirmations like,

I write well and easily. My work is infinitely publishable

I am a great writer, deserving of praise

I always complete the stories I start

You might feel silly saying these things to yourself. No matter, the subconscious does not discriminate. Say these things often enough and your deeper mind, where your dreams reside, will start to believe them.

On a more practical level, train yourself to write short pieces that are self-contained. That is, they have a beginning, middle and end, but are only perhaps one paragraph long.

The trick is to start small. Even just a couple of sentences is enough to begin with. Take simple ideas and write them down. For example, you could write a few lines on making a cup of coffee or catching a bus to work.

When you've put down the key elements you wished to record in a short piece of writing, go back and tighten up the words and sentences, edit until the rhythm of the piece hums. Hemingway used to recommend this practice to new writers.

Do this for at least a dozen short pieces before you tackle a longer work. This simple exercise will help unblock your creativity and put you on the road to success.

Finishing is the key. Get used to writing END after a piece, no matter how short. This is a good way of teaching your brain that you always *complete* your written tasks and later, your more involved projects.

Time Management

In order to write well and effectively, you will need to set aside adequate writing time. Again, this may seem obvious. However, I've known many people who call themselves writers but who simply don't have the time to write. Or they don't schedule time in their lives to write. They bemoan the fact they never seem to get anything much down on paper.

Many writers complain they're blocked but what they really mean is that they're not deliberately setting aside time to write. They say they're waiting for inspiration - and that when it strikes then they will find the time. But any professional will tell you this is not how it works. You can't wait for inspiration. You need to be writing first, and then hope that inspiration strikes you while you're writing. That's the right way round!

Many would-be writers think that dashing off one-thousand words during a rainy Sunday afternoon a few years back qualifies them for the title of *writer* - when in reality, this is simply a lie.

Writers write. Regularly. If you're not writing regularly, you're not a writer. If you're blocked, you're not writing, therefore you're not a writer. Once you understand this idea, you'll appreciate that there's no such thing as writer's block. You're either a writer or you're not.

And when you're a writer, you put time aside to write. Got that?

Nothing too onerous at the start: say an hour a day. Or half an hour if that's all you can manage. Rhythm is the important thing. Writing thrives on routine. Writing two-hundred words a day is much better than writing fourteen-hundred words once a week, or four-thousand words once a month.

Set up a time every day, ideally the same time, that you know you must do some writing, and your subconscious will begin to look forward to those times and perform accordingly. And writer's block (which doesn't exist anyway) will become a thing of the past.

When you're not sitting at your writing desk, make notes during the rest of the day about things you might want to write about. At the beginning of a writing session, get out those notes and add flesh to them. This is always a good way to start, rather than trying to launch into a new project by staring at a blank screen.

I use a few programs for making notes. *Evernote* is good because I can tap ideas into my tablet which are automatically whisked off into the stratosphere and downloaded onto my main computer the next time I log in. *Evernote* is free and I recommend it.

I use all kinds of writing pads too, *Post-It* notes and sometimes even the back of my arm. Anything that's handy.

When you're at your writing desk, never stare at the wall or out of the window, waiting for divine intervention. I know this is the cliché you see in Hollywood movies but, take it from me, it is the worst habit you can develop as a writer. Not only is it not productive, it sends all the wrong signals to your subconscious. When you're at your writing desk, you're there to write. Got that?

Always write *something*, even if it's trivial and lackluster. Professional writers rarely wait until they *feel like it*. Every writer's hero, Stephen King, says you should write even if it feels like you're wading uphill through crap, because writing is often better looking back. Get used to writing the first notion that comes into your head. This process is good practice and will stand you in fine stead when you're writing much longer projects.

Your eventual aim is write just a little faster than the rate at which you think. Get used to preparing for that eventuality now by writing down the thoughts you receive as they arrive in your head. Many great writers attest to the idea they do not write per se: they are merely vessels through which the writing flows. This is because, in reality and in practice, your subconscious is producing the writing for you. All you have to do is to keep up!

You should also train your mind into writing specific pieces over particular time-frames. One short story a week, for instance. Or a longer time span if need be. Whatever you feel most comfortable with is ideal at first. Just so long as you state tangible goals to yourself and commit to them.

Belief

It's vital to engender a sense of purpose for your writing. For a long time I've been aware of a curious phenomenon. That when we truly believe something is possible, it invariably manifests. And the time it takes to manifest is often dependent on:

1. How much work we put into it and

2. How strong our belief is.

This is not because *believing* necessarily makes it so, but that once we commit to an idea of how our reality should be, then we'll often keep working until that reality eventuates.

So, decide now *why* you want to write short stories.

Is it to entertain and enlighten others, or is it something more personal? Do you simply need to satisfy a vicarious desire to write? Are you trying to vanquish some inner demons? Or do you, like me, feel incomplete unless you're continually creating something from nothing?

From now on, meditate on these issues for a few moments every day – perhaps when you wake in the morning or before you fall asleep at night. Plant some seeds of purpose into your subconscious mind and let the motivation, and the commitment to act on your goals, follow through and bubble up into your conscious mind.

When you identify a good, urgent reason, or set of reasons, write them down and carry them with you as a kind of mission statement. Put them on a piece of card and keep them in your pocket or in your bag or on the home page of your mobile. Read your mission statement often, say five or six times a day for a couple of weeks.

Goal Setting

When you've finished a few practice pieces and you're sure you can successfully move on, start to set concrete goals. For instance,

I will write 500 words every day for a week

I will write a 1000-word article and will write nothing else until it's done

I will do brief character outlines for my next short story

Focusing on goals is the first and last step when it comes to achievement.

Nothing can happen in your life without you first identifying what needs to be done and then believing that you are capable of seeing your goals through to completion.

When you've done all of the above exercises and know in your heart that finishing a short story is well within your grasp, only then is it time to move on.

PART TWO:

THE BASICS

Inspiration

Inspiration is not an object or a substance. It doesn't reside in little boxes in the attic. It's not something you can pluck from the refrigerator. It doesn't live under rocks or grow on trees.

If it's anything at all it is an electrochemical reaction in the brain, usually sparked by seeing, feeling or imagining something from a new perspective. In all likelihood it's a re-routing of the synapses that enables the brain to make connections of two or more disparate concepts interwoven or related in an apparently new way.

Whatever it is, it's personal.

It's certainly nothing you can predict nor rely on. And while it's true that an inspired thought can launch a good short story, a novel or even a series of books, you should get used to the idea that inspiration is not all that essential to the creative process.

At least at the beginning of your career.

Inspiration tends to strike you most *during* the writing process. The more often you write therefore, the more often you have inspired ideas. This is as it should be. There's something about the practice of writing that reorganizes thought patterns in your brain. Writing helps the mind carve new pathways and create moments when disparate ideas are held up for review simultaneously, leading to that all important flash of inspiration.

However, sitting around and waiting for inspiration is not to be encouraged. For one, it doesn't work. And two, you could die waiting.

Yes, feeling inspired has the advantage that it can kick start you into proceeding on a course of action, whether it be writing or some other activity. However, *waiting* for inspiration before you act is a mistake.

For a start, you could have a long wait. Inspiration is notoriously unreliable.

For another, although an inspired thought can give you the feeling you're doing something original and important, short story editors will tell you that this is largely an illusion. They rarely see anything they might call 'original'.

In reality, no matter how profoundly you are moved by the notion your idea is unique and far-reaching, it's very unlikely that it is. Because every time you think of a good idea, given the size of the planet, you can assume that about a million other people have simultaneously had exactly the same thought. Now, even if only 1% of those blessed with this new insight are writers they will also, like you, want to write it down and get it published!

It's what Carl Jung, the psychoanalyst, called *synchronicity* - a concept which attempts to explain the phenomenon whereby several people try to get the same idea published at the same time. This happens in science, in Hollywood and on editors' desks every day.

So, if that's the reality, you might be asking, is it worth coming up with original ideas? The short answer is: *no, it's probably not.*

Besides, I guess much depends on your definition of originality. An editor's idea of it is probably quite different from your own. Most of us think that an original idea is one that doesn't seem to have occurred to other people - a clever plot twist or a new type of character or a fresh concept for a story. We then think we must get this idea out quickly before anyone else thinks of it. But as I've explained, that's an unlikely event.

An editor's idea of originality is more rooted in a writer's *approach* to an otherwise unoriginal story idea. For example, the average writer thinks there's nothing much original in writing about vampires. However, Stephenie Meyer's publisher thought that writing about teenage vampires the way she did was wonderfully original. Stephen King, of course, had already written about teenage vampires years earlier but, apparently, Stephenie's originality was in her unique handling of the unoriginal premise.

Clearly, what *can* be original and unique is your slant, your style of writing and your own interpretation of an otherwise good but well-worn idea. Because, if you are true to yourself, explore your idea thoroughly and have faith in your own unique vision, you then become original.

Subject Matter

What interests you? Is it people, facts or plots?

You can approach writing stories from many angles. However, those that are character-based first are usually the most successful.

In whatever you're writing, think of characters as your starting point. Never try to bolt a set of characters on to an existing plot-line as this rarely works. Characters have a habit of taking over a storyline and will often begin to dictate how the story goes. If you fight this tendency and force your characters into decisions they wouldn't naturally make, you'll often end up with a story that doesn't work well. And usually you won't know why until an editor returns your story with a note saying something like: *I didn't believe in your characters.*

The best idea in the world for a story is only as good as your characters. Good characters can save an average story idea. But a great story idea can never be saved by badly drawn, inconsistent characters.

The thing is, too, you don't have much time to impress a reader in a short story.

You must grip a reader - and editor - quickly and the easiest way to do that is to create a likable protagonist or compelling character right up front. If an editor likes your central hero from the start, and believes a reader would too, you're at least halfway to getting your story published.

Sometimes clever plots can eventually make good short stories - especially in the *Science Fiction* genre - but if the resulting story doesn't involve credible people that inspire empathy or what we call *identification*, the story will often come across as hollow or contrived.

Similarly, a few well-chosen or interesting facts, whether historical, scientific or perhaps mundane can make for an interesting framework on which to hang a story. But, without involving personalities, the facts alone will not entertain for long.

As I've said many times elsewhere before, without compelling characters, there's no story. Therefore it's crucial you spend time working on your fictional personalities and on making them real to you and, more especially, the reader.

You don't need to be a master-psychiatrist or a sociologist to identify what's interesting about people. Even the most casual observer of humankind can garner enough information to create a reasonably believable character.

Protagonists don't have to be heroic leaders or beautifully attractive and talented.

The best short stories are rarely about big issues or profound truths. Indeed, simple tales that highlight human traits or foibles in a sensitive and appreciative way are the ones that tend to engender our deepest sympathy.

When you're wondering what would make a good subject or character for a story, don't always try to go for weighty 'significance'. Look too at the trivial, the ornery, the average man or woman in the street - and how they might deal with a slight change in their perspective.

To remind a reader of a simple truth can be much more moving than trying to tackle the esoteric or explain the meaning of the universe.

Genre

Many novice writers begin by believing that writing stories has something to do with coming across as *literary* in some way. They might expend much energy in creating beautiful descriptions of a landscape or the weather. They might spend oodles of time telling the reader about some complex sequence of emotional beats hidden within pages of dense exposition. They might feel the need to explain oceans of back-story, switching point-of-view without thought, before they finally get on with the tale itself.

I think this happens because many classic authors appear to have done this before us. We're taught at school about one-hundred-and-fifty-year-old fiction and have come to believe that's how it's done. And perhaps we grow up feeling that we can't be great writers unless we can emulate these outdated techniques.

This is misguided thinking - and should be avoided.

The 'greats' like Dickens, Tolstoy and Jane Austen were basically *experimenting* with a relatively new form of expression that we now, for convenience, call literary fiction.

They were learning how to use the medium most effectively.

Like us, they were trying to tell stories. And to do it to the best of their ability.

But fiction writing is constantly evolving. We write differently now because we have discovered that when newer rules are applied, the fiction becomes *even more effective* than it was, say, a century ago. These days, fiction moves faster, is more instantly engaging, doesn't flip from inside one character's head to another, and generally holds the interest in a more compelling way because, even in the last one hundred years, we've *evolved* as readers - as well as writers.

It's a mistake to think that all you need to know about fiction writing is contained within the books of those that are considered 'the classics.' Whilst many 'old' books can make fascinating and insightful reading, your job as a *modern* fiction writer is to learn all the 'new' rules that apply to our current age: to create fiction that seems fresh and *relevant* to today's reader.

Plus, the fact is there's very little demand out there for what is considered literary fiction. Most magazines - online and off - publish, and prefer, genre-based fiction.

To many new writers, genre writing (romance, thrillers, horror, fantasy and science-fiction etc.,) is more often than not seen as 'less real' and as such perhaps a product of lesser minds, equated with 'selling out' or writing to a formula.

This is a strange attitude considering most of the best-selling authors of our time are in genre. Look at the work of John Grisham, Dan Brown, Stephen King, Stephenie Meyer, EL James, Patricia Cornwell, Kathy Reichs, Dean Koontz, JK Rowling, Danielle Steel, James Patterson et al. They are all essentially very well-paid genre writers.

And to reiterate the point I made in the introduction to this book, there's a good reason why the most successful writers of our age are writing genre fiction. Yep, you guessed it, because it's what readers want.

And if readers want it, so do short story editors!

Perhaps 'literary' implies something altogether more noble, deeper and more challenging. However, in my humble experience, many writers effectively hide behind their literary label to excuse their lack of success - and talent. They maintain their principles won't let them write 'that sort of thing.'

The truth is, of course, that genre-fiction is actually *harder to get right* than most any other kind of creative writing. It's going that extra mile. The writer of genre not only knows how to write, he or she knows also how to tell stories within a specific framework. The genre writer understands that personality, place and plot – and knowing how to effectively combine those elements in a way that a reader appreciates and enjoys – can be just as important as having something interesting to say and writing well.

Of course, whether you want to write literary or genre fiction will depend on your personal temperament and preferences. But, let me say this now, if you sincerely want to write for publication, and be paid well for your efforts, your wish to indulge in literary fiction may well have to take a back seat - for the time being - to the needs of your target markets.

Because the only surefire way of getting published in a particular magazine is to study the stories they publish, and then write in that style. And perhaps 90% of all the available short story markets are genre-based.

So if you sincerely want to get published, you're gonna have to write genre.

This might seem as the ultimate in 'selling out' but if you want to be a successful, full-time writer or even just get a few stories published, it's most likely what you will need to start doing right now!

But fear not, it really does work.

Editors know what they like and they know what's right for their magazines. And simply put, if you write what they need to publish, they will want what you write.

Take a chance and swallow your pride. Don't fight the market. Write for the market. Why not? You could spend years submitting your own literary stories, wondering why you never get published. Many people do, with no luck whatsoever.

Editors might think your work is wonderful. But they can't publish stories that are not right for their readers. The authors they publish closely study their markets and their editors. If you want to be pedantic, yes, in effect, professional writers often write to order.

But that's the essential difference between the amateur and the professional. This one little compromise to your principles could be your key to success.

Because it's not selling out, it's cashing in!

Scope

Having read this far, ask yourself again, right now, *What sort of stories do you want to write?* And in which genre?

Are they grand sweeping adventures or minute tableaux of passing moments? Most likely they're somewhere in between.

For most short stories, you don't want anything too grand or overly ambitious. You only have a few thousand words (often a lot less) to get across your story succinctly. Too much detail and a yarn will drag. Too little action and dialogue and your editor will probably not make it to the end. Conversely, too many scenes and the editor will get lost and most likely bored or confused.

When you're toying with ideas, remember that you don't want huge dramas spread across generations. You certainly don't want affected language or verbosity. You don't want any unnecessary back-story clogging up the page or lots of static information imparted with no real enthusiasm or directness.

All of these faults will get your MS heading for the return envelope faster than the time you spent licking the stamp!

Always endeavor to imagine your stories simple in scope and theme, precise in direction, as well as easy and fun to read.

Getting Ideas

Ideas are as unique as your own personality. Not all writers will regard what you think is a good idea as a suitable reason to write. This doesn't matter. What does matter is that *you* find it a good reason!

Many writers will tell you they get ideas from all sorts of places.

•*Overheard conversations*

•*News items, movies, TV*

•*Your own life incidents*

•*Other writing/writers, books, magazines*

All of these are valid, especially if you use your imagination to embellish on them. Make notes on ideas that occur to you. Write down snatches of conversation. Keep a notebook to record quick plot ideas. Describe interesting people you meet.

Don't get too carried away with the notion that you must have a complete story idea before you start making notes. Many stories start from the humblest of beginnings.

PART THREE:

CONSTRUCTION TIME

The 7-Step Story Generator

If you're stuck for ideas, don't panic, try this foolproof strategy for coming up with a story.

1. Create 1 to 3 interesting characters

2. Describe their personalities, characteristics and their agendas

3. Make their individual goals at odds with the other characters'

4. Start making notes on how your characters interact

5. Explore how each of the characters will achieve their goals

6. Let your characters suggest the story, easily and naturally

7. Stop when you have a story idea.

The above exercise should take you about ten minutes to half an hour. At the end you should have an interesting scenario that will often develop into a good short story. If not, try it again with different characters.

Do a few of these exercises, for practice.

Characters

I only endorse one way of writing stories.

Characters first and every time, and in a short story, as few as possible. More than three to five get hard to follow. If your story idea contains more than five characters, consider cutting a few out. If you don't know how to do that, try creating what Hollywood calls 'composite' characters. You might have, say, a sister, a best friend and a doctor that all need to give advice to your hero. Roll all three characters into one.

This is an especially useful technique when it comes to novels and screenplays, where character numbers can quickly get out of hand.

Creating good, strong and believable characters is your number one priority when it comes to fiction writing. As a habit, you should spend time developing them, writing out their histories and goals etc.

For the purposes of the short story, you usually don't need too much detail.

Characters don't need to be as fleshed out as you would require in a larger work. Too much depth, as in conflicting emotions, deep psychological traits and more than one 'initiating event' are generally inappropriate for a short story and might detract.

Take one of your characters and do a shorthand sketch of their:

1. Physical attributes

2. Psychological attributes

3. Nationality

4. Age

5. Profession

6. Two important goals

7. Personal traits or talents that might help or hinder those goals

Finally give him/her a name.

Note: Don't name your character too early on. It can color your creativity.

You should find the above list is more than enough to add flesh to characters and is perhaps more than you will need to mention in your story.

Use any spare time you have getting to know your characters. This practice is more important than any plot consideration or story invention. Trust me. You are more likely to be rejected because your characters are one-dimensional and unconvincing than if your plot is bad.

How to Create Instantly Compelling Characters

A character's individual agenda will usually become what drives your story but first you need readers to care about your hero. So what can you do to make your characters instantly compelling?

Sympathy

Readers often root for characters that are innocent victims – or who are subjected to forces that are beyond their control. The girl running from the psychopath or a lost child, or an employee set upon by her boss, or a man struggling against the natural world. Even a nun or a prisoner. All of these characters have the ability to instantly elicit sympathy from the reader.

Jeopardy

People like to identify with characters in danger. Think James Bond or Harrison Ford at the beginning of *Raiders of the Lost Ark*. Although the viewer has no inkling of the character's personality the first time they meet him, they want him to escape / beat the bad guys and triumph.

Jeopardy works for any character involved in a life or death situation. Whether it's Clarice Starling at the beginning of the book *Hannibal* – she's FBI but that doesn't stop her from being terrified of an upcoming shootout. Or Stephen King's *Carrie*, where a teenage girl is taunted by her schoolmates for having her first period in the famous shower scene at the beginning of Brian de Palma's movie (based on the book of course.)

Likeability

Ideally your character should be instantly likeable. It's hard not to root for someone who cares for the sick or lets an old lady have a seat on the bus.

Show your character being kind – don't just say, *He's kind and caring*, your reader won't believe it unless you show the teacher helping a student, or a father coaching his son on how to ride a bike.

Open with the Character

As I mentioned above, it's hard for us humans not to like the first person we're introduced to. James Herbert, the British horror author, used to play with this aspect of our expectations in his novels. He would show the reader a character, describe him in detail and just when you liked him the most, Herbert would kill him off! A clever twist on the guidelines – but I wouldn't recommend you do it too often!

Skilled Individuals

People are naturally drawn to characters that are obviously good at what they do. Have you ever wondered why you might identify with a bad guy who is a good killer, a thief who succeeds in stealing a fortune in jewels, or a computer hacker that can bring down the CIA's mainframe? These are all examples of how we automatically admire great skill in others, no matter how nefarious.

Of course the same rule applies if the character is a good guy, using his skill to the benefit of others.

Familiar Settings

Deep down, we all want to believe we're the same and possess the same values. We treasure life, freedom, choice and the right to live our lives in comfort. At the beginning of a story, we like to see people doing ordinary things and living a good life (at least for while, until it gets boring.) You'll probably have noticed that this is how the majority of horror stories start: the happy family, the good life, the innocence of youth etc. Horror stories use this convention because it's a very powerful way of drawing the reader into a highly believable situation before the 'unbelievable' happens.

Flaws and Foibles

This was one of the first pieces of advice I got from a literary agent: *Make your characters quirky*, he said. Of course I took it to heart and made all of my characters slightly odd with irritating personal habits.

I think the trick is not to go over the top and present slight flaws and charming foibles that will endear your reader to your characters.

Superheroes

We should accept that there's something about the idea of having superhuman powers that intrigues us as a species. Perhaps it's related to prehistoric myths when gods allegedly roamed the planet – or perhaps it's more down to earth than that.

Maybe as humans we always aspire to be more than we are and like to identify with being a superman or wonder woman – though why we need snazzy costumes to appear impressive is anybody's guess!

Be the Reader

One of the simplest ways of drawing in a reader is to tell the 'I' story. First person is eternally compelling but new writers often misunderstand why this is.

When a reader reads a story from the perspective of the writer, they are not generally identifying the writer as the kind of person they can relate to. No, in essence, they become the *character*. They share his or her worldview while they are reading. The character is the reader.

Many writers shy away from revealing themselves in writing but, counter logically, revealing your deepest and darkest thoughts is what the reader wants in order to fully identify with the 'I' character.

However it should be remembered that, when writing from the first person point of view you, the author, should *not* be in the story. The reader is only interested in the character – and ultimately only in him or herself in your character's shoes.

Character identification is part of a sacred pact between an author and the reader. The good writer understands that it is not the story or your writing that is important. It is the reader's eagerness to become your character that defines your skill as a writer.

Character Motivation

When you've done all you can to make your reader love, or at least identify in some small way with, your hero, you can then begin to deal with motivation: outer and inner.

The outer journey is concerned with the story, the plot, the events that drive characters to act as they do – and how they interact with each other. This is largely agenda driven. If Terry wants a new car but his wife Sherry wants to save the money for a holiday, you have two characters whose agendas are at odds. At the simplest level, your protagonist wants to save the world and the bad guys want to destroy it. This is all outer conflict – the drama that drives your story.

The inner journey is more personal. It is what happens to the character's inner world as he makes changes to his life to incorporate the outer journey.

Interactions

Once you have two or three characters you like, write some dialogue between them. Make sure their personal agendas are at odds with each other. If it feels right, make them violently disagree with each other. These conversations should be dramatic, each one playing devil's advocate with the other's point of view. That's the idea. If there's too much agreement between your characters, you story will most likely be dull.

Make notes about your characters' relationships with each other. Establish what they are to your satisfaction before you move on to:

Story

Once you know your characters well and you like the way they interact, start to think of how their relationships might evolve into a plot.

Start with a simple idea and see how far you can push it. Think laterally but don't force your characters into saying or doing things that seem unnatural for them. Your characters must remain consistent. It's okay to put them into situations that are unfamiliar but they must react to those situations with veracity.

And remember a golden rule: they must already have the necessary attributes to escape or overcome any and all obstacles you place in their way.

Creating a compelling story is about taking characters with an agenda and placing obstacles to those agendas in their way. This is how compelling fiction works. If it is not hard for a character to overcome his or her obstacles, there's no story worth telling.

I have courses that explore these fundamental issues in far more depth. *The Art of Story* is one and *The Writer and The Hero's Journey* is another. Here is not the place to duplicate these detailed investigations into the nature of fiction. Suffice it to say that, if you wish to deepen your understanding of how effective fiction is constructed from the ground up, I recommend you read these courses. They're both now available on Amazon.

For the purposes of writing effective short stories however, the steps I have outlined above are sufficient for your short term needs.

Setting

You may have already had some idea where you are going to set your story. Think hard about it now. Is there some reason why it has to set in a particular place? Perhaps you could transplant the action to somewhere else in time and space. There's no real limit.

But perhaps you have a thrilling tale that pivots on a local quirk of law in Cuba, for instance. All well and good, as long as you've been there and can write about it convincingly.

Remember, in your story, setting is often another character. It is as important to your story as the characters within it because location gives people context and can ideally be used to heighten drama and tension.

The 5-Point Plot Structure

Think back to the essays you did at school. This was the basic structure:

1. *Terms of reference*

2. *Agenda*

3. *Premise*

4. *Discussion*

5. *Resolution*

Well, this was how we did it at my school. Perhaps yours was different. No matter. A good short story follows the same kind of format.

1. *Opening sequence*

2. *The central idea*

3. *Obstacles*

4.   *Overcoming*

5.   *Close*

Use this structure to outline a story idea. Remember, keep it simple. Don't use up hundreds of ideas in one story. Use just one or two, that's all you need. It'll help give your writing room to breathe.

Style and Tone

About now, you're probably itching to get started on a short story. Hold back for a little longer. You have a few more decisions to make.

How are you going to write your story? What style are you going to employ? Short sharp sentences? First person and personal? Or moody with lots of description? Chatty and informal? Dark and/or gothic?

Rather than agonize over these decisions, go with whatever you feel you can sustain for a whole story. Your style should be easy and consistent. Don't take on a tone of voice that's not natural to you.

Decide now to write your story as fast as you can in your own voice, without any affectation.

Editors often complain that stories from new writers seem to change tone or even direction halfway through. This phenomenon is usually caused by taking too long to write a story, or by leaving long gaps between writing sessions. For many reasons that I explore fully in *The Easy Way to Write a Novel,* you are literally a different person each time you sit down to write… and it inevitably shows.

Also, writers tend to change their minds about a story as they go along. Not good.

Professionals know that consistent tone is a must for each short manuscript. If a story is not convincingly told in one voice, then later, when you edit, you must take out everything that doesn't fit.

Better to do it right first time. Pick an easy and natural style and stick with it.

Point Of View

Pretty soon you'll need to decide from whose point of view you're going to be telling the story. It's best to stick with just one – your hero or heroine – for a short story. Too many points of view in a story and you're going to confuse the reader.

That doesn't mean you can't have more than one character, only that the world can only be seen through the eyes (and feelings) of one. Be careful not to read the thoughts of others in your story. It's easily done but the 'modern' way is increasingly to tell stories from only one point of view at a time. The practice of what's known as 'head-hopping' is to be discouraged (with, if it was up to me, prison sentences.)

Now too, will be the time to decide whether you're going to be telling the story from the first person, that is, an 'I' story.

'I' stories work well for the first time writer. You may encounter some plotting problems though. Mainly because the protagonist cannot witness events he or she is not directly involved in.

Experiment to see what's right for your story.

Tense

Tense can make a huge difference to a story.

The classic way to tell stories is 'immediate' past tense. This has become the norm. It's so common that readers take it for granted. Although technically the events are over and gone, readers feel they are right there as they are happening.

I'd advise to stick with past tense for ease of storytelling.

Present tense can be arresting, though sometimes it's just annoying. Use it sparingly. Also, unless you're careful, it can be difficult to maintain without accidentally slipping back into the past tense.

I've worked with many new writers who have trouble distinguishing between tenses. They will write in the past tense for instance and, in order to make the action seem more compelling, will switch to present tense. This is bad writing technique until you know what you're doing. For the sake of your first short story attempts, stick with just one tense religiously.

Plotting

Here we create your five-point story plan.

Take a piece of paper, write START in the bottom left hand corner and END in the top right. Draw four vertical lines down the page, so that you end up with five sections. At the top of these sections put the numbers one to five.

Write a *Story Statement* beneath the word START. Your story statement is a short sentence describing what your story is about, its theme, point or premise.

Now write a sequence of five simple plot points going across the page. This is a physical representation of your story. Does the tension and excitement escalate as you move from left to right? It should.

If not, rearrange your plot points so that the story intensifies towards the end.

Keep changing and rearranging your five plot points until you're sure your story is the best it can be.

Under each plot point, make notes, add details. Give weight to the emotional 'beats' that matter by imagining them, seeing them as events in your mind's eye. Then write down what you see - in note form.

Consider deleting events that do not seem important to the thrust of the story. Do the same with characters. Can your story be told without certain characters altogether? Can two become one? Can several become a composite?

Are you duplicating plot events? Remember, the simpler the story the better. Like a good joke, it's brief, nothing is wasted and every line is there for a reason. Here's some great advice: *If in doubt, cut it out.*

Now, just under the word END, write your twist.

That's right. Sorry to spring that on you suddenly… but that was intentional.

The Twist

I'm going to let you in on a secret now. Whatever happens in your plot or your story, in order to make your work infinitely more salable, you must have a twist. Especially one that nobody saw coming. What better way to achieve that than to imagine a twist even you didn't see coming at the beginning of this plotting exercise?

The twist is the secret weapon of the intelligent author. Editors – and readers - love them. They are satisfying. They show cleverness. They show that you, the writer, have a complete grasp of the short story medium.

With this simple technique, you show you don't just make things up as you go along, or that a particular story isn't good because of some fluke. You've shown you can prepare and synthesize a whole story before you start. With this one little trick, you mark yourself out as serious about your craft. You come across as the consummate professional.

Why? Because, as any good editor knows, the only way to have a good, convincing twist at the *end* of your story is to know what it is before you started writing. Because only by knowing your own twist can you now deliberately write the whole story steering the editor / reader away from guessing it!

When a short story editor gets to the end of a story and realizes he has been to some extent 'duped' by your writing skills, he/she is impressed and instantly considers you a superior writer, and one to watch.

So, if you want to be a paid writer quickly and often, implant this simple message into your brain:

There must be a twist at the end of your story AND you must know what it's going to be before you start writing.

Your twist may be thin and flimsy, it could be profound, it may be enigmatic. It can cause a smile, a smirk or just raise an eyebrow. It doesn't matter too much, as long as it's there.

Trust me on this.

Building a Template

Take your five plot points and your twist from the previous exercise. Copy them (in their most effective order) and list them down the left-hand side of your word processor screen.

Put spaces between them.

In the spaces, fill in the gaps between the plot points with any action, scenes, dialogue cues and other information you think you will need to take you smoothly from one plot point to the next. Don't put in trivial actions like waking up, bathing, going to the shops and eating meals unless they have a direct bearing on the story.

When you've finished you should have less than a page of notes, but hopefully everything will be in the right order.

This is the template you will use to write your short story.

You need this because as you write, you won't get stuck because you will always know what comes next.

And don't think you can shirk on this.

I've lost count of the number of times writers email me to say, *Yeah, I understand the template idea but, Rob, I don't work that way. I like to make it up as I go along.*

And so I patiently respond with some encouraging words and respectfully reiterate my belief in the fiction template, knowing that my words are falling on deaf ears.

And then, I wait.

Yep, and almost every single time it's these same writers who get back to me and say, *Oh, hi Rob, um, I'm about two thirds of the way through and I'm kind of stuck, um, I don't really know where to go with this story now.* You have no idea how hard it is to hold back saying, *I told you so!*

Really, making it up as you go along is fine for amateurs. Or for professionals who know exactly what they're doing. But when you're starting out, you need a plan.

The '1-2-3-Bang' and Other Stories

At this point you'll be getting an idea how long your story will be.

In most instances you will be writing to a pre-determined length set by publisher's guidelines.

Here's a quick overview of modern short story lengths:

Flash Fiction is usually between fifty and two-hundred words long. The medium is becoming more and more popular as, supposedly, the attention span of the average reader diminishes. Some blame TV. Some blame the Internet. I blame the magazines and websites themselves.

When you read a magazine or e-zine filled chockablock with ads and articles that are designed to entertain and divert you in the shortest time possible, why would readers want to linger over a page full of dense text? Flash fiction assumes we don't have time to read. This is clearly a nonsensical idea. Otherwise, why would novels still sell in their millions?

Ah well...

Mini stories usually come in at around a thousand words. Modern *True Love* or *Romances* fall into this category and follow a formula which I call the *1-2-3-Bang* format, as in,

1.   *Obstacle*

2.   *Obstacle*

3.   *Resolution?*

BANG: The twist.

Most serious magazine fiction is between one-thousand to three-thousand words. Anything up to three-thousand words should ideally not have much in the way of a subplot. It's too confusing when most editors are looking for a linear sequence of events leading to a logical conclusion.

In most *Story Magazines*, as in publications specifically designed to carry short stories, you can usually write up to five-thousand words, sometimes up to eight-thousand depending on the publisher. These stories will perhaps contain one subplot or some item of interest outside of the linear format.

Anthologies and *Short Story Compilations* can carry stories up to ten-thousand, even fifteen to twenty-five-thousand words - but you usually have to be a 'name' to get all that space in a book!

These latter publications are commonly printed by independent editors licensed through a major publisher. Contrary to the way it can appear, the editors of these books don't usually scour magazines for good stories to republish. They usually release a 'call for submissions' to recognized and dependable authors, agents and reputable writers' associations. The authors then submit work which may or may not have been published elsewhere.

Note: Even then, these authors will only submit work to the guidelines in the 'call for submissions' or else write specifically to fulfill them. Even the pros do it right. But then, that's probably how they got to be professional in the first place.

Anything over between ten-thousand and fifty-thousand would more commonly be called a novella. Anything beyond that is a fully-fledged novel, and outside of the remit of this book.

PART FOUR:

WRITING YOUR STORY

The Opening Paragraph

Prepare yourself for a shock. After all your hard work, thought and inspiration, an editor will rarely read more than your opening paragraph. Sometimes not even that.

They simply don't have the time. Besides, to their way of thinking, the first paragraph is your opening gambit, it is your attempt to snag a reader's attention. If you can't do that, or don't even try, why would the editor think the rest of your story is worth reading?

Your opening is the most important part of your story. Without a good opening, you're dead in the water.

And yet good openings are hard to get right. That's why it's worth spending time on them, even after you have the story completed. Always go back to the beginning and ask yourself if the opening sentence is strong enough.

Your opening should be intriguing. It should place a question in the reader's mind at once, even if it's, *'What's going on?'*

The 'real' start of a story is also one of the most difficult things we writers have to identify. The standard advice is this:

Start writing, working your way into your story with ease and confidence. Then, when you go back, you'll probably find your 'real' intro somewhere around two-hundred to four-hundred words in. Authors are notorious for wanting to set everything up before a piece of drama. In a short story, you don't have time to set up anything. It's a luxury you can't afford. Besides which, readers are generally smarter than you think.

Too much setup is boring anyway. Learn to throw readers right into the action with a compelling statement or perhaps a strong piece of arresting dialogue. Whatever you do, don't start a story with a long sentence about the countryside or the weather. A good editor will not read on. Not because your story will be bad necessarily. He might think your words are very well-chosen and apt.

However, he will also know that you have not made a special effort to impress with the start of your story.

He'll know that you're an amateur who hasn't grasped this one simple rule: the opening should grab a reader by the lapels and force him or her to read the rest of the story!

Fast Writing

Before you start a writing session, do this simple meditation exercise. It works wonders.

Close your eyes, relax and breathe deeply. Say to yourself:

With every word I write I become more calm, confident and creative.

Repeat the phrase three times, with feeling. Imagine yourself writing quickly, fluidly, smiling to yourself, enjoying the simple pleasure of creating words.

Trust that your subconscious will write for you, that it has the ability to come up with all the ideas and words that you need. Tell yourself you won't question what you write. Let go of your conscious, logical mind. Believe it is possible to write quickly and easily this way.

When you open your eyes, write without thinking.

If you do this for ten minutes, at first, I think you'll be amazed at the result.

Get Ready... Go!

The key to creativity is a healthy mental state. Your subconscious writing ability is much easier to access if you are relaxed and clear.

If you use the conscious, logical side of your mind to write, you'll take forever, as in the traditional image of writers, agonizing over every word. You may have been doing this for years already and find it a difficult habit to break.

If so, you must learn to change.

Writing with your logical mind not only wastes your time (it's not particularly productive), it can actually harm your creativity. What the ego, your self-esteem and your career needs are results and quickly.

While you are writing, try to switch off your conscious mind. The way to do this most effectively is to write fast. Don't edit, don't go back, and don't think about anything but the next line. Let your fingers write automatically.

Don't look at the screen too often. Look at the keyboard.

Try it. At first it may seem disorientating but stick with it. It's exactly the right way to increase your output.

Where before you might have written two-hundred words an hour, this one technique can usually increase your output by around ten times!

But the thing that will surprise you the most is that, contrary to what you might expect, your writing won't be all that bad. Why? Because your subconscious is in control. You may make spelling mistakes and makes lots of formatting errors but, trust me, when you're in the flow, your subconscious won't let you write badly!

The subconscious mind has infinite knowledge, talent and genius that are far superior to anything your logical, rational self can muster. If anything, you might discover that you have a style different from the one you were used to. I promise you it will be better, more fluid, more in tune with the way your mind works. Plus, it will no doubt be a lot easier to read.

The trick is to write your entire short story this way, fast and furious. No going back to look at anything, or to edit or improve the text. No. Commit yourself to writing the whole story first, without pause.

Even if you're writing in short bursts of half an hour or so every day, when you come back to write, don't go back and edit, don't look at what you've done previously. This habit will slow you down.

During your writing sessions, don't give yourself time to think. Just keep your fingers tapping the keys. If you think you're going to run out of things to say, look briefly at the next line on your template and write the first thing that comes into your head. Yes, the first thing, anything. It doesn't matter if it's unrelated.

Whatever you do, don't stop. Don't correct spelling mistakes or grammatical errors. Just keep going.

Go for it. This is the 'easy way' to get your first draft done quickly.

And when you've done that, then you can get straight on to…

The Second Draft

This is where your story starts to take its final shape.

First, go back through your MS correcting the spelling and grammatical mistakes. That's all. Leave the rest.

Read it through quickly. Is the sense of the story you wanted to write there? Does it prove your point, show the premise, illustrate your theme?

If so, good.

Next, cut out any passages that have no direct bearing on the thrust of the story. Murder your darlings. As the late great Elmore Leonard said, *Remove anything that sounds like writing.* This might be hard. If you can't bear to lose some of these passages, cut and paste them on to another document.

You can always use them for something else later.

If there are any obvious gaps in the storyline, do quick bursts of fast writing and slot them in to the text. Keep this process going until you have the 'shape' and 'balance' of the story right.

Editing

When you've finished the entire second draft, that is, when you can't think of another thing to add to improve it, when it seems to have a solidity of its own, stop, give yourself a pat on the back and reward yourself in some way.

Next, put it away for a week and work on something else. Later, pull it out again and start the final editing process.

Go from each sentence to the next making sure everything makes sense. Note the rhythm of the words and sentences, give them appropriate weight and significance but don't forget that the object of the exercise is to transfer the meaning of your story into the mind of a potential reader.

To do that you must be clear: in your imagery, in your scene-construction and in your choice of dialogue, right down to the symmetry of each paragraph.

When you're sure you've got the sense right, see if you can't cut out some more words. You'll find you can generally strip away fifteen to twenty-percent of all the words in your story to make the whole manuscript tighter and less verbose. Take out any and all lines that don't push the story forward.

Remember another golden rule: There was no story ever written that did not benefit from being shorter! Even by just a few words.

This process may take a few hours or a few days depending on how much reworking you're doing. However, as you progress, you should feel a growing sense of creating something solid and perhaps important.

Now have a look at the opening of your story again.

Does the first line do your tale justice? Is it strong enough? Does it grab your reader and make him or her ask questions?

Keep editing away, making the opening gambit tighter than anything else in the story. Strip down the adverbs. Remove the passive. Be bold.

Formatting

If you haven't done so already, format the document.

Use double-spacing for the text with an inch and a half (three to five centimeters) of blank space on either side and at the top and bottom. Left justify the text. Center the title. Put page numbers at the top right-hand corner along with your name and story title (shortened if necessary).

12-point Times New Roman or 10 point Courier are the industry standard fonts. Don't try to do clever things with fonts. Don't capitalize to add emphasis, ever.

Polishing - The Final Edit

Give the finished manuscript to someone whose judgment you trust to read it and make appropriate comments. Preferably give it to two. These are called 'beta readers' in *Kindle* speak.

You'd be surprised at the mistakes you leave in no matter how hard you try not to. It's one of the curious tricks the brain plays. After about three passes, your brain corrects the errors: you literally don't see the mistakes.

If you edit on the screen, always print off a version and read it on paper for errors. The change of medium tends to override the brain. Most professional authors check a hard copy of their work before they send out anything for publication.

Get into the habit. It's important.

Get your two chosen beta readers to mark all spelling and grammar errors in red pen and to make comments about what they haven't understood or thought was dull and uninteresting.

When you've got their comments back, go for a final polish.

Look closely at the comments your readers have made. Take their suggestions onboard but go with your heart with things that are important to you.

If both critics agree on a particular point, carefully consider what they're saying and make the necessary changes. If they don't agree, you're probably safe to leave it in. You can't please everybody.

The process of polishing is harder for some authors than writing the first draft. Some writers agonize over every word and phrase, wondering if they've got it right. That's all good up to a point - as long as you know when to stop. Some writers just can't stop, can't let go. Basically, these writers probably fear criticism and ridicule. This is a very common ailment for new writers. Even seasoned writers.

It's something you have to get over by realizing that generally readers don't care about your writing per se – they're usually only interested in what you're writing about. It's a tenuous difference, of course, but one that can release you from years of self-doubt if you fully grasp the meaning of it. Besides, it's natural to feel a little insecure about your writing. It's actually a function of your right-brain to criticize, and to logically analyze your work. It does so by picking holes in everything – just to let you know it's doing its job!

To a certain extent, fear of criticism gets easier with practice. Confidence sets in when you receive validation for your writing. A time comes when you realize you were much too hard on yourself in the first place.

Here's a great tactic: When you edit your work, calm your conscious mind, place your faith in the subconscious and polish to the best of your ability. Don't question what you've done. Don't over-analyze and dissect every sentence and paragraph if you feel you're not helping the story. Do too much editing and polishing and you'll end up with something flat and lifeless. Short stories need to feel fresh. Consistency is often more important than overt cleverness or literary merit.

At the end of this process, try reading parts of your story out to yourself, making sure they flow, are easy to read and hopefully entertaining. When you think the whole story works to the best of your current ability, stop.

You're done writing that story.

PART FIVE:

SUBMITTING YOUR WORK

Presentation is Key

When submitting to editors and publishers you need to think in terms of having a 'submission pack', which will include the following:

1.   *Your introductory letter (or your email cover letter)*

2.   *Your MS*

3.   *SASE & postage (assuming it's not an online submission)*

Introduction Letter

This is the first thing your recipient will look at. It's therefore imperative you make this slick, professional looking, and in faultless English.

Always use clean white paper in letter or A4 size. Never use colored paper or weird fonts. If your home printer is not printing cleanly then get it fixed, or have the letters and your manuscript printed at a local photocopy shop.

Remember: Don't send anything through the mail you would not want to receive!

You need say very little in your cover letter or email. Any more than one-hundred words is excessive. Just introduce yourself, your story and state that it is offered for publication, and in what territories. A long author bio is unnecessary for short story submissions. Your merit is judged on the story, not your career (or lack of it.)

In the US, you will be offering First North American Serial Rights (FNASR).

The technical terms don't matter. The editor is really only

interested in whether your story has been published before, and where in the world.

If you can, only offer your stories for sale to one country at a time. This is becoming increasingly difficult with the onslaught of globalization, as many publishers want world rights. If that's the case, try to limit the amount of time they can keep the rights to your story.

Many Internet e-zines will only want rights for a few months, a year maximum. Beware of publishers who want all rights forever. It's unfair and can severely limit your earnings!

Unless you have something riveting to say in any future correspondence with editors, keep your further messages short and sweet. Never try to sell your stories or yourself or your enthusiasm, or explain something you feel readers should know about you. If your manuscripts don't work on their own terms, without any prior introduction or embellishment, you shouldn't be sending them out!

You are free to send out your story to as many editors as you like and don't let anyone tell you any different. Given the inefficiency of most publications, it's unreasonable for a publisher to expect you to wait for a reply before you send out your submission to another.

The only rule is that once your story has been accepted, you should tell any other publishers that might have your story in consideration that it is no longer available.

Rejection

This book is about getting your work taken seriously. However, for even the best and most professional storywriters, rejection is par for the course.

One surefire way to cut down on your rejections is not to send your manuscripts to editors who won't be interested in them. This sounds obvious but is apparently the most common cause for rejection.

Before you send out your story manuscript, make sure you have studied the magazine, know the guidelines and feel in your heart that this particular magazine editor is exactly the correct recipient for your story.

You could be right. However, you may still receive a rejection. Never mind. There are a million and one reasons for getting your work rejected and only one or two of them will have anything to do with the quality of your work (if you've followed the advice I've given you!)

Whatever you do, don't take rejection personally. Easy to say I know. It's hard not to take rejection badly. The only cure is to get used to the feeling. It dissipates over time (but never completely leaves you.) One acceptance often makes it all worthwhile.

Don't lose heart.

If you're sure the magazine is right for your material, then send out another story straightaway. Editors like persistence and enjoy seeing work from the same author – especially if improvement is apparent.

This is how I got many of my own stories published: by immediately sending out another on receipt of a rejection from a particular editor. They seemed to like persistence in the face of discouragement.

If an editor has made suggestions to make your story better, make the changes and send your manuscript back promptly.

Editors particularly like writers who heed advice and learn from criticism. Because they know that it's those writers who take onboard suggestions and improve that generally become the professionals.

Rights & Payment

When an editor accepts your short story, he/she will normally let you know within around four to six weeks, sometimes longer. E-zine publishers may get back to within a week or so.

When they get in touch, they will usually state the payment rate, the date of proposed publication and the rights they want. If you're happy with the terms, sign and return anything they require immediately.

Don't think this an excuse for you to start a new friendship. It's not. Keep everything as professional as necessary. And get back to your writing, because this is the only thing they're expecting of you!

Examples of Short Story Writing

If you're looking for models of good short story writing, get hold of some compilations by the following authors. They are all masters of the craft. Read them and learn from their techniques, especially characterization, pacing and their specific use of words.

Agatha Christie

Arthur Conan Doyle

Clive Barker

Daphne du Maurier

Edgar Allen Poe

Ernest Hemingway

Faye Kellerman

F Scott Fitzgerald

H G Wells

Jeffrey Archer

Jonathan Kellerman

Mark Twain

Philip K Dick

Ray Bradbury

Somerset Maugham

Stephen King

Ursula K LeGuin

Conclusion

I hope this book provides you with solid steps on your road to regular publication. It's an attainable goal for any and all writers, as long as they keep learning from criticism as well as praise. In this business, we have to keep improving. It's a lifelong exercise.

Ideally, if you aspire to make a living from writing one day, you could do worse than aim to write a short story a week and get into the habit of sending out your manuscripts as you write them. Try to have something out and being considered permanently, if at all possible. It will make you feel better and ensure your success in the long term. Keep a log of which story is where, who rejected or accepted what and especially try to learn from the stories that are published. After all, if you're doing something right, you'd do well to keep doing it!

Best of luck. And don't forget to let me know about your successes! In fact, any feedback is welcome. In the mean time,

Keep Writing!

Rob Parnell

The Easy Way to Write

SHORT STORY MARKETS

Please note that short story markets tend to come and go like the wind. Sometimes good markets dry up, restrict their submission periods or eventually die altogether. Also note that not all short story markets are paying markets. Most would like to be but some need you to understand that running a magazine is a tough, time-consuming, and often expensive business. You will need to be patient and understanding when dealing with these resources.

The listings here are correct and current at the time of publishing this book. Please email me if you find that any of the links are broken or that the market has disappeared - or if you hear of a hot new market. I will make regular changes to the listing based on your feedback.

Thanks.

Email me here: rob@easywaytowrite.com

AE: The Canadian Science Fiction Review

http://aescifi.ca/

Alfred Hitchcock Mystery Magazine

http://www.themysteryplace.com/ahmm/guidelines

Analog Science Fiction and Fact

http://www.analogsf.com/information/submissions.shtml

Apex Magazine

http://apex-magazine.com/submission-guidelines/

Arc

https://arc.submittable.com/submit

Asimov's Science Fiction

http://www.asimovs.com/info/guidelines.shtml

Baycon Program Book

http://baycon.org/guidelines.html

Beneath Ceaseless Skies

http://beneath-ceaseless-skies.com/page.php?p=submissions

Boys' Life Magazine

http://www.boyslife.org/about/contributors/writers.pdf

Buzzy Mag

http://www.buzzymag.com/submissions/

Cemetery Dance Magazine

http://www.cemeterydance.com/extras/category/guidelines/

Chiaroscuro Magazine (ChiZine)

http://www.chizine.com/submissions_fiction.htm

Clarkesworld Magazine

http://www.clarkesworld.com/magazine/submissions/

Cosmos

http://www.cosmosmagazine.com/contact/submissions/

Cricket

http://www.cricketmag.com/pages_content.asp?page_id=25

Crossed Genres Magazine

http://crossedgenres.com/submissions/magazine/

Crowded Magazine

http://www.crowdedmagazine.com/guidelines.php

Daily Science Fiction

http://dailysciencefiction.com/submit

The Dark

http://www.thedarkmagazine.com/

Dark Discoveries

http://darkdiscoveries.com/

Ellery Queen's Mystery Magazine

http://www.themysteryplace.com/eqmm/guidelines

The Magazine of Fantasy & Science Fiction

http://www.sfsite.com/fsf/glines.htm

Flash Fiction Online

http://www.ralan.com/m.flash.htm#FlshFctnOnln

Glimmer Train Stories

http://www.glimmertrain.com/writguid1.html

Grantville Gazette

http://www.grantvillegazette.com/

Grave Tales

http://www.cemeterydance.com/extras/grave-tales-comic-guidelines/

Highlights

http://www.highlights.com/contributor-guidelines

IGMS (Orson Scott Card's Intergalactic Medicine Show)

http://www.intergalacticmedicineshow.com

Lightspeed

http://www.lightspeedmagazine.com/guidelines/

Lore

http://www.lore-online.com/

Nameless Magazine

http://www.namelessmag.com/

The Night Land

http://www.thenightland.co.uk/nightficoff.html

Nightmare Magazine

http://www.nightmare-magazine.com/guidelines.html

Odyssey: Adventures in Science

http://www.odysseymagazine.com/pages/contact.asp

One Buck Horror

http://www.onebuckhorror.com/

The Pedestal Magazine

http://www.thepedestalmagazine.com/submitguidelines.php

Penumbra

http://musapublishing.blogspot.com/p/penumbra.html

Phobos Magazine

http://phobosmagazine.com/

Playboy

http://www.playboy.com/

The School Magazine

http://theschoolmagazine.com.au/

Shimmer

http://www.shimmerzine.com/

Shock Totem

http://www.shocktotem.com/

Strange Horizons

http://www.strangehorizons.com/Guidelines.shtml

Tor

http://www.tor.com/page/submissions-guidelines

Universe Annex

http://www.grantvillegazette.com/Universe_Annex_Submissions

Unlikely Story

http://www.unlikely-story.com/?page_id=4

Waylines Magazine

http://www.waylinesmagazine.com/

Wily Writers Speculative Fiction Podcast

http://www.wilywriters.com/blog/ -

Zoetrope: All-Story

http://www.all-story.com/submissions.cgi

Abyss & Apex

http://www.abyssapexzine.com/submissions/

Aurealis

http://www.aurealis.com.au/

Cosmos Online

http://www.cosmosmagazine.com/contact/submissions/

Gud Magazine

http://www.gudmagazine.com/subs/submit.php

Heroic Fantasy Quarterly

http://www.heroicfantasyquarterly.com/?page_id=39

Ideomancer

http://www.ideomancer.com/

Interzone

http://ttapress.com/interzone/

Lamplight

http://lamplightmagazine.com/submissions

Michael Moorcock's New World's Magazine

http://www.newworlds.co.uk/

Midnight Echo

http://midnightechomagazine.com/

On Spec

http://www.onspec.ca/submissions/

On The Premises

http://www.onthepremises.com/

Spinetinglers

http://spinetinglers.co.uk/SubmitStory.aspx

Star*Line: Digest of the Science Fiction Poetry Association

http://www.sfpoetry.com/

The Strand Magazine

http://www.strandmag.com/

Andromeda Spaceways Inflight Magazine

http://www.andromedaspaceways.com/

Betwixt

http://www.betwixtmagazine.com/submissions

Beware The Dark

http://sstpublications.co.uk/sst/Magazines/BTD-
Submissions.html

Birkensnake

http://www.birkensnake.com/submit.html

Breath & Shadow

http://www.abilitymaine.org/breath/write.html

Electric Spec

http://www.electricspec.com/

Electric Velocipede

http://electricvelocipede.com/

Expanded Horizons

http://www.expandedhorizons.net/magazine/?page_id=5

The First Line

http://www.thefirstline.com/

Fried Fiction

http://www.friedfiction.com/

Innsmouth Magazine

http://www.innsmouthfreepress.com/

Interstellar Fiction

http://www.interstellarfiction.com/

Kaleidoscope

http://www.kaleidotrope.net/

Leading Edge

http://www.leadingedgemagazine.com/

Neo-Opsis SF Magazine

http://www.neo-opsis.ca/

The New Bedlam Project

http://newbedlam.com/zine/?page_id=579

Newmyths.com

http://www.newmyths.com/

Perihelion Science Fiction

http://www.perihelionsf.com/

Phantom Drift: Writing the Weird, Wyrding the Word

http://www.phantomdrift.org/

Plasma Frequency Magazine

http://www.plasmafrequencymagazine.com/

Postscripts to the Darkness

http://www.pstdarkness.wordpress.com/

Scape

http://www.scapezine.com/index.php?p=1_5_Submissions+

Scheherezade's Bequest

http://www.cabinetdesfees.com/scheherezades-bequest/

Shadows & Tall Trees

http://www.undertowbooks.com/

Shroud Magazine

http://www.shroudmagazine.com/submissions

Space & Time

http://www.spaceandtimemagazine.com/

Spellbound

http://eggplantproductions.com/?page_id=656

Sterling Magazine

http://sterlingmag.ca/

Tales of the Unanticipated

http://www.totu-ink.com/guidelines.phtml

Three-Lobed Burning Eye

http://www.3lobedmag.com/

Ticon4

http://ticonderogaonline.com/

Untied Shoelaces of the Mind

http://www.untiedshoelacesofthemind.com/index.php#Submissi

ons

ZYZZYVA: the journal of west coast writers & artists

http://www.zyzzyva.org/

Cyborg Anthology (untitled)

http://www.ralan.com/m.antho.htm#CbrgAnthlgy

Snafu

http://www.ralan.com/m.antho.htm#Snf

Strength From Within

http://www.ralan.com/m.antho.htm#StrngthWthn

Fractured

http://www.ralan.com/m.antho.htm#Frctrd

Coffee

http://www.ralan.com/m.antho.htm#CffUFO

All Hallow's Eve

http://www.mysteryandhorrorllc.com/submissions.html

Anthologybuilder

http://www.anthologybuilder.com/guidelines.php

Epic Saga Publishing Anthologies
http://www.fitz42.net/epicsaga

Razor Thin Studios Anthologies
http://razorthinstudios.weebly.com/submit-to-rts.html

Satan's Toybox: Toy Soldiers
http://angelicknightpress.com/

Static Movement Anthologies
http://www.staticmovement.com/

Tales of Fortannis: 3
http://michaelaventrella.com/2013/06/04/submit-a-story-for-the-next-tales-of-fortannis/

Thirteen Volume Three
http://www.13horror.com/

Undead of Winter
http://www.mysteryandhorrorllc.com/submissions.html

Weird Legends
http://ataleforatale.com/2013/04/08/weird-legends-submissions/

Whortleberry Press Anthologies
http://whortleberrypress.com/

Ralan
http://www.ralan.com/

Absolute Write forum
http://www.absolutewrite.com/forums

Abyss and Apex
www.abyssandapex.com

Andromeda Spaceways
www.andromedaspaceways.com

Angels on Earth
http://www.angelsonearth.com/writers_Guidelines.asp

Aurealis
www.aurealis.com.au

Dark Discoveries
142 Woodside Drive
Longview, WA. 98632
USA

Dirt Rag Magazine

www.dirtragmag.com

Duotrope's Digest

www.duotrope.com/

Espresso Fiction

www.espressofiction.com

Freya's Bower

www.freyasbower.com

Fly, Rod and Reel

www.flyrodreel.com

Firefox News

http://tinyurl.com/22jcw8

Grass Roots Magazine

http://www.grassrootsmag.com/wrgu.html

Jim Baen's Universe

www.baensuniverse.com

Les Bonnes Fees

http://www.les-bonnes-fees.com/guidelines.html

Over My Dead Body

www.overmydeadbody.com

Postcards From...

http://postcardtales.blogspot.com

Redstone Science Fiction

http://redstonesciencefiction.com/guidelines/

The Rose & Thorn Ezine

www.theroseandthornezine.com

The Thyazine Foundation

world@thyazine.org

Short Bread Stories

www.shortbreadstories.com

Second Story Press

http://www.secondstorypress.ca/submissions

Quill Pen Press

http://www.Quill-Pen.net

Vestal Review

http://www.vestalreview.net/Guidelines.html

Winning Writers

http://www.winningwriters.com/

Wet Ink

http://www.wetink.com.au

Zoetrope: All Story

http://www.all-story.com/submissions.cgi

ROB PARNELL'S WRITING RESOURCES

Free Writing Lessons and articles

http://easywaytowrite.com

The Easy Way to Write a Novel That Sells

http://www.amazon.com/Easy-Write-Novel-That-Sells-ebook/dp/B00FR155MU

The Writer and The Hero's Journey

http://www.amazon.com/dp/B00I9N879Q

The Easy Way to Write Romance That Sells

http://www.amazon.com/Easy-Write-Romance-That-Sells-ebook/dp/B00FEM9MQW

The Easy Way to Write Thrillers That Sell

http://www.amazon.com/Easy-Write-Thrillers-That-Sell-ebook/dp/B00G3DBC2S

The Easy Way to Write Crime Fiction That Sells

http://www.amazon.com/Easy-Write-Crime-Fiction-Sells-ebook/dp/B00F83EH2G

The Easy Way to Write Fantasy That Sells

http://www.amazon.com/Easy-Write-Fantasy-That-Sells-ebook/dp/B00FML0V8S

The Easy Way to Write Picture Books That Sell

http://www.amazon.com/Easy-Write-Picture-Books-That-ebook/dp/B00G1XIUF2

How to Write a GREAT Children's Book

http://www.amazon.com/Write-GREAT-Childrens-Book-Easy-ebook/dp/B00EV5CD14

The Easy Way to Write Horror That Sells

http://www.amazon.com/Easy-Write-Horror-That-Sells-ebook/dp/B00GX2B29M

The Easy Way to Write Hollywood Screenplays That Sell

http://www.amazon.com/Easy-Write-Hollywood-Screenplays-That-ebook/dp/B00GR0D1YE

Show Don't Tell

http://www.amazon.com/dp/B00IF63F9O

The Art of Story - Writing Fiction That Sells

http://www.amazon.com/dp/B00HV69CJQ

Anatomy of the Modern Bestseller

http://easywaytowrite.com/DDbestseller.html

The Nuts and Bolts of Writing

http://easywaytowrite.com/DDnutsandbolts.html

Easy Cash Writing

http://www.amazon.com/Easy-Cash-Writing-Living-Freelance-ebook/dp/B00JLJFO1G

Wealth from Words

http://wealthfromwords.com

The Write Stuff

http://easywaytowrite.com/the_write_stuff.html

Self Editing for Success

http://easywaytowrite.com/DDediting.html

Character Creation

http://easywaytowrite.com/character.html/

Plotting 101

http://easywaytowrite.com/plotting.html

Write From The Start

http://easywaytowrite.com/Write_From_The_Start.html

Write to The Top

http://easywaytowrite.com/Write_To_The_Top.html

The E-Files

http://the-e-files.net

CONNECT WITH ROB PARNELL

Easy Way To Write Blog

http://easywaytowrite.blogspot.com.au/

Rob's Author Blog

http://robparnell.blogspot.com.au

Rob's Youtube Channel

http://www.youtube.com/robparnell2008

Rob's Twitter

https://twitter.com/robparnell

Rob's Facebook

https://www.facebook.com/rob.parnell

https://www.facebook.com/rob.parnell.106

Rob's imdb

http://www.imdb.com/name/nm1239587/

Rob's iTunes:

https://itunes.apple.com/us/artist/rob-parnell/

114

ABOUT THE AUTHOR

Rob Parnell has been writing fiction since he was five years old.

Born in Winchester in the UK, he lived for a long time in London, pursuing a music career until, suitably chastised for his impertinence, he moved to Adelaide, Australia, where he now teaches writing and success strategies to his many thousands of subscribers.

His preferred genre is the thriller - sometimes with a supernatural edge - in which he writes short stories, graphic novels, YA novels and adult thrillers.

Rob has written over fifty non-fiction self-help titles and been published all over the world for the last fifteen years. Also a composer, singer, music producer and budding movie maker, Rob is ecstatically happy to be married to Robyn Opie Parnell, his savior and the popular bestselling children's author.

www.ingramcontent.com/pod-product-compliance
Lightning Source LLC
Chambersburg PA
CBHW021209290526
45796CB00006B/36